Contents

Introduction	4
Sheet 1	5
Sheet 2	7
Sheet 3	9
Sheet 4	11
Sheet 5	13
Sheet 6	15
Sheet 7	17
Sheet 8	19
Sheet 9	21
Sheet 10	23
Sheet 11	25
Sheet 12	27
Sheet 13	29
Sheet 14	31
Sheet 15	33
Sheet 16	35

 *Introduction*

With a lot of worry and fear in the world today, it is important to be informed and make good decisions based on the facts at hand.

Panic buying caused supply shortages for some products. In Australia, one of the bizarre products to fall to panic buying was toilet roll.

This little book, produced as a light-hearted response, offers a "Never Run Out" reminder that there is always an alternative.

Contained in this book are sixteen "sheets". It may be single ply, but we are sure you will agree the 70lb paper has plenty of bulk!

We all have a roll to play!

NEVER RUN OUT

Lou Papier

Single ply 70lb sheet

NEVER RUN OUT

Lou Papier

Single ply 70lb sheet

NEVER RUN OUT

Lou Papier

Single ply 70lb sheet

www.ingramcontent.com/pod-product-compliance
Lightning Source LLC
Chambersburg PA
CBHW040244010526
44107CB00065B/2870